The Art of Africa:

TRIBAL MASKS

The Art of Africa:

TRIBAL MASKS

FROM THE NÁPRSTEK MUSEUM, PRAGUE

ERICH HEROLD • Photographed by JINDŘICH MARCO

PAUL HAMLYN • LONDON

TEXT BY ERICH HEROLD
PHOTOGRAPHED BY JINDŘICH MARCO
TRANSLATED BY TILL GOTTHEINER
GRAPHIC DESIGN BY J. MARCOVÁ

Designed and produced by Artia for
Paul Hamlyn Ltd
Drury House · Russell Street · London, WC2
© 1967 by Artia

Printed in Czechoslovakia by Polygrafia, Prague
S 2243

Introduction

When at the beginning of our century a group of Parisian artists discovered the art of Negro Africa for themselves, and thereby for the general public, it was received with great interest by all manner of creative artists and people of culture. Previously this art had been the exclusive domain of ethnographers and curators of ethnographical collections in museums. Quite naturally, this interest did not rise in a steady curve but had its culminating points and periods of apparent stagnation. As a result this interest is sometimes labelled as a fashion, a vogue of exoticism, primitivism, and so on. It does contain certain elements of this in some strata. But I would hardly dare use the term 'fashion' for a phenomenon which has lasted for six decades, is taken up by every new generation and shows, generally, a rising trend.

While at the beginning of the century Africa was still an exotic, mysterious and inaccessible continent, it has ceased to be this in our time, in the period of highly developed air traffic, tarmac roads and television, a time when the representatives of the African states themselves participate in international negotiations of every conceivable kind. At least in this sense the exotic aspects of African art have ceased to impress anyone who admires this art. Interest in African art, in other words, is no fashion. Nor can the term fashion be applied, on a similar level, to modern European art which, at the beginning, marvelled at the works of African and Oceanic artists and was influenced by them.

This creative contact between the art of different continents is proof that at a vital moment two related spheres of different ages met face to face, to whom life had presented identical questions, questions to which the younger of the two had already found the answer. It was L. Segy in his book African Sculpture Speaks *who, in the author's opinion, came closest to the truth when he spoke of the anxiety and fear of modern Man, fear that arises from the split or conflict between the intellect and emotion in our life. From this he deduced that modern Man derives aesthetic satisfaction from African art on account of its directness and emotional depth. It should, of course, be realized that the fear and anxiety of the African arising from his powerlessness and dependence on Nature is different from the fear of a member of twentieth-century civilization, which arises from the split of his intellectually saturated and emotionally starved personality, and from the contradictions of modern society and technical civilization. The encounter, therefore, was only a momentary one, because the answer to the involved questions of today is inevitably more complex than the answer that Africa once found for its infinitely simpler situation. The truth of this is confirmed by the subsequent development of modern art since the beginning of this century. But we shall probably keep returning to the original art of Africa as an elementary source of emotional satisfaction.*

In African art dance and ritual masks form an important element. The mask, of course, is not an exclusively African feature. It is found all over the world. It plays an important role in the culture of most Oceanic peoples and in that of the original inhabitants of the north-western coast of America. Masks are known from ancient and present-day Central America. In comparatively recent times the world got to know masks belonging to the tribes of Central India. They were known in palaeolithic Europe, as shown by the well-known painting of a masked magician in the Trois Frères cave in France. They have survived down to modern times in the folk culture of some Central European nations. But nowhere do masks seem to have spread so far nor to have achieved such wealth of form as in Africa. The mask reveals the artistic and creative strength of the Africans. It is this that attracts our attention. At the same time the mask helps to realize religious ideas and uphold traditions of social norms. This is foremost in the case of the Africans, though both aspects are indivisible. If we are to comprehend the artistic quality of masks, their hidden meaning and function, this second aspect must be borne in mind.

In other words, the mask is linked with African religious and social life. True enough, that today it sometimes serves as a form of entertainment for spectators: for example, the *mashamboy* masks of the Bakuba, or the comic masks in which boys of the Bayaka tribe in the Congo dance in front of spectators after finishing 'school in the bush.' Even here the masks were originally a means of upholding social authority and an expression of sacred tribal traditions. When wearing his mask the African does not represent a supernatural being. In the eyes of his fellow-tribesmen the supernatural being really exists and becomes embodied in the mask throughout the time of its appearance. Therefore the mask is inviolable and the least infringement of the rules surrounding the mask is strictly punished by the community, sometimes by death. Masks play an important role in secret societies, which are widespread in many parts of Africa. They are formed of the most important members of the tribe, who through such an organization see to it that the traditional tribal rules and morals are upheld. They, in fact, represent a police and legal authority. Their influence is decisive in the religious and social life of their people. The members of the secret societies appear in masks during initiation ceremonies, or at the funeral of one of their members, for on such occasions the danger from the influence of evil spirits increases and the masks serve as protection against their power. Masks are used wherever evil spirits can be shown to have caused harm to the community. In such a case the mask of a kindly spirit helps to discover the guilty and prevent the further extension of evil. Masks further embody the gods of fertility who may influence the abundance of the harvest. And masks embody the spirit of the deceased who through the masks can speak, for a last time, to their descendants.

Appearances in masks are almost exclusively confined to men. Women are not even allowed to set eyes on certain of the masks under threat of punishment. Others serve to drive women away from the camps in the bush in which young boys are prepared for their initiation. Women wearing masks are very exceptional, existing among the Mende tribe, in Sierra Leone, and in Liberia where there is a women's secret society.

The mask itself covers the face or the entire head of the dancer. The rest of the body is covered in long flowing fringes of raffia palm fibre or strips of bast; sometimes, as among certain tribes in the Congo, it is clothed in tight garments made of string net.

In the Cameroons the masks are dressed in long flowing robes of cloth. On some masks,

8

especially those in more recent collections, long fringes have survived which covered the body. On the majority of them, however, the existence of such fringes is indicated merely by rows of tiny holes along the edge of the mask. In some places, for example, among tribes living on the Ogowe River in Gaboon, masked figures walk on stilts. Their appearance is accompanied by the sound of rattles and drums or horns, and sometimes the masked figures themselves made supernatural noises with the help of small instruments. In our collection such an instrument has survived inside a mask from the Bajokwe tribe in the Congo, used for guarding the camp of boys undergoing initiation (plate 48). This consists of a short hollow wooden cylinder with a tight membrane which produces sound.

———

This book, as will be explained below, naturally does not include all types of masks of all African tribes where masks are or were in use, say until the middle of the nineteenth century, that is, prior to the period of intensive contacts with Europeans. Only the main types of the most important areas are reproduced here. In fact, the existence of masks is spread across a vast area along the entire coast of the Gulf of Guinea and Congo, throughout the inland area of the western Sudan and the entire Congo Basin right to the western shores of the Great African Lakes and into the area of northern Angola. It is sometimes assumed that masks are exclusively West African in origin. This is not true. Highly developed masks exist among the Makonde tribe living on the border of Tanganyika and Mozambique, and among the Barotse peoples in southern Africa. We even know of masks made of gourd and cow dung from the Shilluk tribe of the Sudan.

A frequent question raised is that of the age of African masks. There seems to be a romantic idea that what is old is precious. This is, of course, true in some cases, especially when we are dealing with the art of areas where the traditional forms of art have died out or survive only in degenerate form, as a form of tourist industry. But even there it is impossible to deny categorically the existence of artistic quality.

9

How old, then, are African masks? There is no easy answer to this question. Probably the oldest proof of the existence of African masks are rock-paintings in areas of the Sahara that are nowadays deserted, in southern Algeria. These were discovered and presented to the world by the expedition of the French explorer, Henri Lhote. Written documents of their existence also have survived, for example, from some mediaeval travellers who visited the western Sudan, among them the Arab traveller Ibn Batuta writing in 1352. The oldest masks actually surviving date from a slightly later period. They are made of ivory, and represent some of the finest products of Benin art.

The masks found in museums and private collections are only rarely more than one hundred years old. Our knowledge of the age of African masks might well be broadened in the future, for the archaeology of the African continent is still in its early stages. A surprise in this field would, however, only occur if the Africans formerly used different materials than they do today, for masks of perishable material would survive only under highly exceptional circumstances.

With few exceptions, masks are made of wood, bark or other perishable material, and those that are not the prey of the tireless and non-selective jaws of the white ants soon succumb to the moisture of the tropical climate.

The maximum age of masks we know is roughly one hundred years. This does not mean that such age is essential in the case of all examples surviving in good condition. For the existence of some masks was discovered much later, new ones are still being found and, according to Hans Himmelheber, the well-known German investigator writing in 1965 (in a letter to this author), new masks are today coming into being in places where none had existed before.

A layman is often confused in his attempt at judging antiquity by the beautiful patina of some of the masks. This, however, does not depend on the age of the mask so much as on its having really been used during rituals. Such masks are more rare in collections. This is partly because it is easier to obtain a new mask from its maker than from the user of the mask, particularly if it is one that during the ritual was consecrated to embody a supernatural being. As a result some masks that came to European museums during the nineteenth century look quite new, while others, acquired only a few months previously, appear to a layman to be far older objects. By way of illustration I should like to point out that of all the masks published in this book, only five can definitely be said to have been used during ritual ceremonies. Among them belongs the exceptionally beautiful mask from the Guro tribe of the Ivory Coast (plate 13).

In regard to artistic value two matters are decisive: the artistic quality and the perfection of the craftsmanship. Their scientific importance depends mainly on the surviving documentary evidence accompanying them, facts describing all the circumstances under which they were acquired: period and place of discovery, their function as observed by the collector, evidence provided by the maker or user of the mask, etc. Casual collectors, unfortunately, usually disregard this second aspect and in the past it was they who acquired most examples of African art.

Yet the absolute value of the mask depends in equal measure on these two aspects. It might even be said that the second one is more important for an understanding of the meaning and social purpose. Only if we have knowledge of the two aspects can we correctly evaluate the importance of the time of acquisition or purchase. These facts are given in our catalogue, at least in approximation, wherever they survive in museum records.

———

Mention was made above of the importance of material for the survival of masks. The basic material used is wood. The kind of wood to be used is prescribed in tribal tradition and differs from place to place. It is not by any means known in every case what type of wood was used. Some kinds are very hard, others are woods that are light-weight and can be easily shaped. Where soft wood was used for the mask, this causes trouble in collections after a longer period. For even under European conditions they tend to disintegrate. Though little is noticeable on the surface the wood is attacked by insects inside and turns into white dust. This is often not discovered until the mask is subjected to an accidental knock whereupon the mask falls into pieces that even the most skilful of restorers is unable to reassemble: our present knowledge of restoration technique, however, makes it possible to conserve the wood if the deterioration is discovered in time. Soft resins are used for the purpose though this has to be done without interference with the patina of the mask and care must be taken to prevent any subsequent change in colour. Surprising though it may be, museum curators have the greatest worries with masks of hardwoods, which are apparently more resistant to outer influences. Usually these masks are heavy. Their walls are comparatively thick and the comparatively wide range of temperature changes and humidity in the European climate causes unequal pressure along the inner and outer surfaces of the mask. The results are vertical cracks that spoil the aesthetic impression and which are, so far as I know, beyond repair. They can be prevented by regulating the climatic influences on the masks in the rooms where they are kept. African art ignores the principle of unity of material. Hence we find combinations of a wide variety of materials on the masks. They include soft coloured sheet metal, such as copper or aluminium, fur, animal teeth, cock's feathers and human hair, textile, glass or ceramic sherds and cowrie shells. In some areas glass beads are used to cover the entire surface of the mask. In the area of the Cross River on the border between Nigeria and the Cameroons special masks are made in the likeness of a human head. The basis of these masks is a wooden head covered with finely worked antelope skin, treated to resemble parchment. It has been said that formerly human skin from killed enemies was used for this purpose, but I do not know if anyone has tried to prove this assumption by histological research on any of the examples surviving in European collections. Materials of all kinds are also used as complements to the masks.

Wood is, however, not the only basic material in the production of masks. In the southern Congo, for instance, the foundation is basket-work, onto which the face is modelled in

12

a plastic mixture, probably of resin and wax. The Warega tribe in the Eastern Congo makes famous masks from ivory. Others are known to have been cast in bronze, especially in the Cameroons but also by the Senufo tribe of the Ivory Coast. These masks are clearly of more recent origin, and in appearance they are modelled on the wooden masks. On the whole, it can be said that the African maker of masks does not reject any of the more modern materials that can be used. And the use of such materials does not, in any way, lower the value of the mask. For example, the well-known mask of the Bajokwe tribe, which has appeared in many publications, and which belongs to the collection of the Museé de l'Homme in Paris and represents one of the most perfect examples of this type of mask, has a shirt-button on its forehead. It may rightly be assumed that in future we shall see the use of plastic materials on masks.

The surface of the mask is treated further. When we find in collections masks with wood in its natural state, we are in all likelihood dealing with unfinished objects, or with modern pieces made for the tourist market to serve as souvenirs. The mask receives its patina from the carver; that is to say, the surface is rubbed with oil which in time tarnishes so that the mask gives the impression of old dignified bronze. Most of the masks are poly-chrome. Among the better-known masks, those of the Yoruba of Nigeria show outstanding polychromy as do the masks of the Bayaka tribe and the neighbouring Basuku from the Kwango River area in the southern Congo; these masks may each have several colours. The masks of certain tribes can be characterized by typical colours, for example, various shades of brown from almost orange to dark brown for those of the Bapende tribe in the Congo. Colour was often used even in those cases where it cannot be detected at first sight as it gets lost under layers of patina and dirt. But closer investigation usually shows red patches on the apparently monochrome brown-black masks and statues of the Senufo tribe in the area of southern Mali and the northern region of the Ivory Coast.

The colours on the African masks have symbolic significance. This is particularly true of white, the colour of the world of spirits, the colour which people paint themselves with

13

if in mourning or hit by disease. White plays an important role over almost the entire territory over which masks are to be found. The use of blue, which is most frequent, or of green and yellow, which is very exceptional, must be considered due to later foreign influence.

Apart from the colouring matter the African artist in making masks used certain graphic effects. This method is widespread especially among the tribes of the Grasslands of the Cameroons and in the eastern parts of the Congo: the surface of the mask bears a dark patina and the details of a human or animal face are expressed in negative carving by deep notches left in the natural light colour of the wood. By this contrast of dark and light colour the Cameroons carvers achieve a particularly lifelike expression of the mask.

———————

African masks are made and carved exclusively by men; this is part of the strictly applied tradition of division of labour. The creative process itself is a complex ritual. In his work the artist makes very careful preparations, including fasting, purification and abstention from sexual intercourse. During the course of the work, which is done out of sight of accidental spectators, he offers various sacrifices to avoid becoming a victim of the spirit which he summons by this activity (E. Leuzinger, *Afrikanische Skulpturen*, 1963).

The African carver works with the simplest tools. The most used is a long, comparatively wide adze, attached like a small hoe to a long wooden handle. This tool carves the basic shape, including all important details. Marks of this universal tool can often be found on the inside surface of the mask, hollowed for the face or head of its user. More delicate work is carried out with an ordinary knife and the final touches before the patina is added, or the colouring applied, are usually made with a piece of broken glass, which helps to smooth out uneven surfaces. It is remarkable how the African carver can achieve such results with these simple tools.

He uses an ordinary knife to make dense rows of fine notches, used on the masks to indi-

14

cate hair or the fine lines of tattooing on the face. He does not use shaped chisels to ease his work as his European colleague would, who by the very use of these more perfect tools reveals that he is attempting to make fakes. The European plagiarist cannot normally compete with the African artist as to patience and time.

The marks of tools used during production are not the only signs that show fakes. In more recent times the use of more sophisticated tools can be found even in the work of African carvers. As a result a more complex judgement of material, formal aspects and other points is required to distinguish the original from its copy.

The African carver burns in some tiny details. Usually this applies to small circular apertures in the ears, eyeholes, scars or tattooing of tribal marks on the faces of masks or statues. Masks, like the figure sculptures, are usually carved out of one piece of wood. There are, of course, exceptions such as in the case of certain tribes who make masks with movable lower jaws, or the well-known highly stylized figures of antelopes used as head-dress masks in the Antelope Dance of the Bambara tribe in the western Sudan. These subtle abstract carvings, particularly where conceived horizontally, make it impossible to make the carving out of one piece of wood, since even careful handling might easily lead to damage. Hence the body and the head with the long horns are carved separately and the two parts are joined at the neck with a leather ring; in more recent works nails or a metal ring is used. Technically, African masks can be divided into several basic types according to how they are worn, or how large a part of the head or body of the user they cover.

The basic type is the face mask. This term shows that we are dealing with masks that cover only the face. It is found almost universally over the entire territory where masks occur in Africa. As was said above, very often fringes and other objects are attached to heighten the effect of the mask and also to hide the identity of the wearer. These masks are attached to the face through the garments that are worn with it, or they are tied on separately. In exceptional cases, especially among the Guro tribe on the Ivory Coast and probably among other tribes of that country, they are held on by the teeth with the help of a hor-

15

izontal bar on the back of the mask (plate 13). This also occurs in the case of the well-known masks of the Gazelle Peninsula in New Britain which are modelled of clay on the facial parts of a human skull.

The second basic type is the helmet mask, sometimes described by different authors as *Topfmaske* (pot-mask), *Glockenartige Maske* (bell-shaped mask), etc. These terms describe the shape of the masks more or less exactly. They are carved out of a piece of tree trunk in the shape of a helmet or bell, the hollow part of which is used to cover the entire head. Widespread though this type is, it is less so than the preceding one. Some tribes, such as the Mende of Liberia and the Basuku of the Congo, use only this type, while among the Baluba, the largest tribe in the Congo, and in the Grasslands of the Cameroons both kinds are known.

In addition, there is a transitional type. Masks which are modelled on the surface with the full front and back parts of the head, but on a slightly smaller scale, so that they cannot hold the entire head of the dancer. This type is to be found among the Gelede society of the Yoruba in Nigeria and Dahomey. The shape of those masks is determined by the way they are worn, resting obliquely on the forehead of the dancer.

Another special type of mask is known from the Niger Delta. The masks represent faces (plate 34), but are intended to be worn not on the face but on the top of the head in a horizontal position, so that they may be viewed from above. They represent water spirits and their bearers are submerged below water during performances so that the faces of the masks alone move on the surface of the water in front of the spectators. Some animal masks found in other regions should be included in this group.

The third basic type is the head-dress mask. They represent entire human or animal heads resting on top of the wearer's head on a small support woven from basket-work or on a wooden cap-shaped support. Important works of this type are masks of the tribes of the Cross River region (plates 35—36). They include also the antelope masks of the Bambara tribe. Unique are the shoulder masks, known only among the Baga tribe in Guinea. They are

16

large wooden female busts with strikingly flat breasts, with the face usually carved in the characteristic style of that tribe, with a large beak-like nose. Such a mask, weighing about 70 kilogrammes (11 stone) rests on the shoulders of the wearer and he can see out through a small window placed in the centre between the breasts.

Less well known are hand masks, among which should be counted the Warega masks of the Eastern Congo, mentioned above. They are held in front of the face. Sometimes those of the Bayaka tribe of the Congo, also belonging to our collection, are wrongly described as such. Masks of this type have some form of handle below the chin which only serves to keep the masks in balance. Basically the Bayaka masks are helmet masks, even though only the facial parts are carved out of the wood.

Mention should be made, for the sake of completeness, of miniature masks, worn or carried as pendants. They include the tiny copies of initiation masks of the Bapende tribe in the Congo, carved in ivory, which are worn by men all their lives on a string on the chest as a symbol of having undergone the initiation ceremony. For their beauty and magnificent patina acquired through the years of having been worn on the skin, they are highly popular objects of collection.

––––––

The artistic style of the masks has been mentioned several times and this term is to be found frequently in our catalogue. The question of style is of great importance in the geographical and ethnical classification of works of art from Africa, in cases where no records of origin exist.

In some cases the question can be resolved by an examination of the material used, as in the masks from the Cross River area; elsewhere the manner of work gives a clue, e.g. basket-work head-covers in the case of masks from the river basin of the Kwango in the Congo; at other times, the social and religious images from which the theme of the mask or the figural sculpture is derived. Examples of this are the shoulder masks of the Baga tribe.

17

A case in point is the mask illustrated in plate 17. At first sight it is striking on account of the tall pillar-shaped protuberance on the top of the mask, surmounted by a miniature human head. Some quite definite idea must have inspired this mask. L. Frobenius in his classical work on African masks and secret societies published a mask of the Kru tribe of the Ivory Coast, which is similar in concept, and yet from the point of view of artistic treatment of the given theme the two have little in common. Both the masks originated on the Ivory Coast so that they must have been based on a related world of ideas, even if they differ in execution.

Within African art styles is a set of traditionally upheld forms whereby the African artist gives expression to the objective and the subjective world of his ideas and the fantasy of the group in which he lives. Individual geographical regions, even individual ethnic areas within those regions, and sometimes individual villages, have a whole vocabulary of abbreviations and symbols, through which the artist expressed himself. The degree of artistic mastery does not lie in the personal originality of the master in the European sense, in his creation of new shapes and the mastery of new themes even though there are, of course, exceptions to this rule; it rested in the originality of the manner in which he used traditional art forms.

African art has countless numbers of such styles. Today we are still very far from knowing them all, and it is highly likely that we never shall. In many cases our retrospective determination of the provenance of objects on the basis of stylistic features cannot lead us beyond the fixing of certain broader regions of style, or their relation to certain better known styles. It may remain uncertain whether we are dealing with local or ethnic deviations of known forms of expression, with various degrees of a conditioned development in time, individual deviations from the tradition, or the personal contribution of the carver. The difficulties of forming a judgement on these facts are caused by our insufficient and unsystematic basic information and the relatively short span of time during which we have been able to form a picture of African art.

18

The situation is further complicated by the fact that we have to assume, even for the recent past, the transposition of themes and shapes among various ethnic groups. This has been proved to exist in a number of cases. Perhaps in no other part of the world have there been so many migrations and overlaps of ethnic groups as in Africa. We have also to remember that individual families of carvers moved from place to place, or that their work was commissioned for other groups.

The question of style is closely related to the 'primitiveness' of African art. What in some cases justifies our speaking of primitiveness in the case of African art is, mostly, not the art itself but the world of primitive images which inspired this art and which it represents. These images are connected with the low state of development of a given society. But the art itself, its crystallized style, the manner in which these images are given shape, are the result of a very long development, the result of centuries of endeavour of many generations trying to gain mastery over the raw material so as best to express their ideas.

That is the reason why that art has such strong emotional appeal for us, too, who live remote from these ideas through the millenia of development of European civilization and the European manner of thinking.

————

This book does not set out to be an exhaustive, representative survey of all that is aesthetically best among African masks. With only three or four exceptions the selection of masks shown in this book was made from one collection, that of the Náprstek Museum of Asian, African and American Culture in Prague.

An exhaustive, representative survey would have to draw its material from the various large and small collections the world over. One collection alone would be insufficient, even if it were the largest and best known ethnographical collection or museum in the world. In my view only five or six examples from our collection would have their rightful place in such a major work, assuming that the number of masks published would be several times

19

as large as those illustrated in this book. Even so, if it were in practice possible to make such a selection the choice would inevitably be influenced by subjective elements. Most of the existing publications dealing with African art adopted this method. Nobody has, of course, attempted to exhaust all existing public and private collections, for an attempt of that kind would be unreal. A number of authors endeavouring to give a survey of the best works of African art have had the opportunity to derive material from the best known West European, American and African collections. This makes it all the more surprising that the choice of individual authors differs little one from the other.

In my view this fact was fittingly described by the Austrian scholar A. Schweeger-Hefel in her work *Holzplastik in Afrika* (Vienna, 1960), where she wrote about sculptures that kept re-appearing in new publications until they became, as it were, paradigms of African art.

The uninitiated might well assume that what exists is being published, and that there is no other material in the collections. In fact, the storerooms of world museums are literally bursting with works of African art, whole series of variants of known and less known types, and it cannot be said that the most interesting and valuable pieces are only those that have appeared in publications. Hidden in the museum storerooms are quite unique examples which have never been published, the works of art of nations and tribes of whose artistic activity little or nothing is known. It is also surprising that in those books that were written on the basis of selection from the world collections there appear side by side quite rare and precious pieces and more average works, or even below average examples of relatively recent origin. Moreover, there seems to be a tradition which deliberately overlooks the highly characteristic work of certain tribes which should be included in surveys. The impression is that the authors intended, by their silence, to keep these matters from their readers.

The purpose of this publication, in other words, is to present to the reading public the most interesting African masks belonging to one medium-sized ethnographical museum and in so doing widen the selection of material that shows the wealth of expression of

African sculpture. We want to show that we are still far from knowing African art in all its outer aspects, to say nothing of its inner meaning, and that a comprehensive knowledge needs to be based on everything that has been saved for the future in the various collections. Naturally there are certain problems that arise from the fact that the selection was made from one collection only, and one that is far from being a large one. There is the question of a certain incompleteness and with it goes a certain lack of balance in the selection. If this book does not include, for example, masks of the Sudanese tribes of the Dogon, Mossi or Bobo, it is due to the fact that these masks do not exist in Czech collections. And if, on the other hand, we include a whole series of masks of the Yoruba of Nigeria or the Bayaka of the Congo, the reason is not that we consider the works of art of those tribes are the most typical for the overall picture of African art, but that the art of those ethnic groups is strongly represented in our collection.

The reader might be surprised that in the case of a number of pieces the exact function and importance is not known. Naturally wherever collections are scientifically established records of time, place and function of collected objects are meticulously kept. Written, and in more modern times, photographic records make it possible to state the function in the environment in which it came into being. A set of such data accompanied by further facts on the articles collected provides a starting point for an understanding not only of African art, but also all further forms and aspects of original, non-disintegrated cultures. Unfortunately, there are sadly few collections in world museums which possess such documentation, and this is particularly true of African art collections.

Most of the objects were collected accidentally or by chance, as souvenirs of the visit to exotic countries, as part of the loot of military expeditions, or they were acquired in large numbers for the European market, for their commercial or aesthetic value.

The collectors had no thought of any further scientific treatment of the objects nor had they any idea that facts on the circumstances of the find and their use are often 'more valuable' than the objects themselves.

These are some of the problems faced, likewise, by our collection as it is published in this book. None of the collections from which the Prague Museum collection came into being was assembled on the basis of really scientific methods of acquisition with the exception of the masks from the Ivory Coast and the Congo. There the collection was undertaken by people who fortunately realized the importance of at least some basic facts on the provenance of the objects they acquired. In all other cases the provenance of the objects had to be determined according to analogical elements of form on the basis of known types.

———

The collection of African masks in the Náprstek Museum in Prague, which forms part of the collection of African art as such, is of fairly recent origin. The museum was founded over a hundred years ago, in 1862, by a Prague citizen, Vojta Náprstek. Although at the beginning there was more stress on Japanese and American collections, and Africa was not strongly represented in the museum, during the nineteenth century two large collections of African ethnographical objects were acquired.

The most important was that of the Czech doctor, naturalist and explorer, Dr. Emil Holub. His gigantic ethnographical collection from southern Africa is today scattered in many European museums. Apart from Vienna, where its largest part is housed, and the Náprstek Museum, where the second most important group of objects are to be found, smaller ethnographical collections of Dr. Holub's acquisitions may be found in Copenhagen, Leningrad, Dresden, Bremen, Stuttgart, Paris and the University of Jena. Unfortunately, the collections did not include any masks from that area. But Holub made drawings of Barotse masks, published by L. Frobenius in his *Masken und Geheimbünde Afrikas* (Halle, 1898). That is the oldest record of African masks in the Prague collection.

The second large collection of African ethnography, the collection made by Staněk in the lower reaches of the Congo, and acquired in the early nineties, strangely enough, does not include any African sculpture or masks.

22

The beginning of the Prague collection shown in this book dates from 1926. In that year the Czech Ministry of Education and Enlightenment purchased for the Náprstek Museum a large ethnographical collection belonging to a private collector, A. Sachs of Jablonec on the Nisa. A. Sachs was the owner of a local glassworks and he was a dealer and exporter of glass beads to various regions overseas. In Africa his exports went to Nigeria. Sachs preferred to collect objects in whose manufacture his glass beads were used. His collection included also many other remarkable original examples of native culture, all of which later passed into the possession of the Náprstek Museum.

From Nigeria this included a comparatively large collection of Yoruba sculpture and masks as well as some masks from the Cross River area. Certain features point to the fact that the collection was acquired before the World War I, probably by the agent who represented Sachs locally. But we do not have exact data on the time and place of collection nor has any further documentation survived.

Nine years later, in 1935, the collection of African art gained further exhibition pieces. That year the museum purchased what has come to be probably its most valuable collection of African art, gathered by Dr. J. Golovin on the Ivory Coast. Golovin was a Russian emigré, a doctor who bequeathed his collection to his brother, a sculptor living in Prague. The collection must have been made in the years after the World War I. Apart from masks, the most interesting examples of which are illustrated in this publication, there were numerous figures. The collection is interesting as it includes a number of unknown or hitherto unpublished types. It gives a deep insight into the complex conditions of works of art on the Ivory Coast. In the case of most of the objects precise data on provenance and sometimes even function have survived in the museum catalogues. They are given in full in this book.

The museum records mainly quote the Bete tribe as the ethnic source. Little is known of that tribe's work, and since some of the museum records are obviously muddled they can therefore not be accepted as completely reliable. The sculptures and masks in our collection

23

which are said to originate among the Bete tribe, form several clearly distinct groups with features of several known styles. It does not seem likely that all these styles flourished simultaneously in such mature form in one ethnic group. Even though there is some doubt as to the correctness of the statement of the well-known French scholar Denise Paulme (*Une société de la Côte d'Ivoire hier et aujourd'hui: les Bété*, Paris, 1962) that this tribe did not produce sculpture and masks, this fact has yet to be put to a critical test.

The sculpture from the Museum in Abidjan, published recently by W. Fagg in the catalogue to the exhibition *Africa: 100 Tribus — 100 chefs d'oeuvre*, is described as a work of the Bete tribe; in style it is identical with some of our pieces from the Golovin collection attributed to that tribe. This shows that some of our masks may, after all, be ascribed to the Bete, after critical evaluation. For that reason I have restricted myself in the masks published here to pointing out elements of style and stating their relationship to a certain known style.

In 1936 the Museum purchased a further collection from the Czech writer Joe Hloucha. It was the first part of his extensive collection which the museum managed to acquire. J. Hloucha was probably the greatest Czech collector of non-European art. As a writer he sought inspiration for his works from the traditional Japanese environment and his interest in collecting was largely centred around Japanese art. He began to acquire objects of non-European art and ethnographical interest in 1898. From the very beginning he paid attention to African art but there can be no doubt that until 1905 he did not possess a single African mask in his collection. In 1929—30 he held a large exhibition of non-European art in Prague, where, in the African section, nine masks were put on show. The exhibition attracted great attention among the Czech public and the press, and voices were raised to the effect that the collection should be preserved as a unit, and that it should be acquired by the Czechoslovak state for public purposes.

Unfortunately, there was a shortage of public funds and, as a consequence, some of the African objects that proved most important and most valuable for research work were

24

sold to Berlin after an auction following an exhibition in Berlin held by Hloucha in 1930. The brief and incomplete data in the catalogue to the exhibition 'Sammlung Joe Hloucha, Prag' are not sufficient for further studies, but they give a picture of what the Prague collections lost by the sale. After 1936 Hloucha sold to the Náprstek Museum some other parts of his collection, especially African works. The rest came to the Museum in 1956, when Hloucha bequeathed all his remaining collection to the Czechoslovak state. As far as we know Hloucha purchased his African objects mainly from the well-known Hamburg firm of G. Umlauff. Like all collections of similar origin this one, too, lacks all facts on provenance, and the origin and function of the objects can only be judged from published analogies. The Museum managed to acquire a few very interesting examples of African masks after the World War II. They had formed part of the relatively small, but very exclusive private collection of non-European art of J. Maternová. This collection, too, lacked all accompanying data. This is all the more unfortunate since it includes a most beautiful mask which in all likelihood was made by the Kalabari Ijo (plate 34). Another mask, resembling those of the Toma tribe in Liberia (plate 2), has no analogy anywhere among the material published. It is a very interesting example, which in regard to the careful treatment, particularly along the back, was clearly not made for the tourist market, and is perhaps a work of art of an unknown people, most probably from Liberia. It was included in this publication, among others, in the hope that it might be possible to find an analogy of which more facts are known.

The collection of masks from the Congo came, with only two exceptions, from the Czech sculptor F. V. Foit living in Nairobi. F. V. Foit set out on a tour of Africa in 1947, in the company of his wife. He was particularly attracted by the work of the local carvers of masks and sculptures in the Congo. He lived for a time among the pygmies of the Congolese forest and made portraits of them. During his journey he acquired a large ethnographical collection which he presented to the Czechoslovak state. Today this collection, with its comparatively careful documentation, forms part of the Náprstek Museum. It is to

Mr. Foit that we owe one of the best collections of contemporary traditional Congolese art. Even if it includes some works made with an eye to tourist demand, as a whole it was selected with profound knowledge of traditional carving and good taste, as the examples included in this book testify. One of the interesting facts in Foit's collection is that some works of African art cease to be anonymous, since in the case of certain masks and sculptures of the Bakuba tribe the collector noted down even the name of the maker. In 1949-50 Mr. and Mrs. Foit collected sculpture in the Congo. One mask from the Wabembe tribe (plate 72) which they presented to the small regional museum in Telč in Moravia, was acquired in the course of a brief visit to the Congo in 1957.

The other masks were brought to Czechoslovakia as souvenirs from various visits to Africa. A set of six masks came from the area of the River Ogowe in Gaboon, two of which are included in this book (plates 38—39). There is an interesting mask of the Bayaka tribe with the figure of a squatting European (plate 67), purchased in the Congo in 1928 or 1929. An outstanding mask of the Guro tribe on the Ivory Coast (plate 13) came to Prague by chance and belonged to the department of Oriental art of the National Gallery in Prague before its transfer to the Náprstek Museum.

One mask which is published as belonging to the region of the Dan tribe (plate 4) originates from the former ethnographical collection of a missionary order from Teplice-Boho-sudov in western Bohemia. This collection, unfortunately now scattered, has no other examples of African art.

———

Mention should be made of the technical aspect of this publication, the illustrations. Before undertaking the job we tried to arrive at a correct method of photographing African masks and African art in general. We examined a number of publications in which objects of African and exotic art in general stood out in the limelight of numerous frontal, side, top and back and additional reflectors like stars on a screen, in places even arranged among leaves of tropical household plants. It is our firm conviction that African art must make its impact upon the spectator and reader through its own image and its own power of conviction and that it does not stand in need of artificial aids. The results of such endeavours never do correspond to the original intentions of the makers of this traditional African art. Spotlights can be used to dramatize even a box of matches. Not that we wish to stop anyone from experimenting. But we think that such experiments should be presented to the reader as experiments in artistic presentation on the part of a certain photographer, not as the art of Africa.

For that reason we decided to photograph the African masks in not very intensive sunlight, at various times of the day, on black-and-white and colour film, and to make the final selection out of a large number of photographs. This approach, and the technical limitation given by the alternation of coloured and black-and-white reproductions in the text caused a certain lack of logical sequence in the geographical layout of the masks reproduced, particularly in the case of masks from Gaboon which precede those from the Cameroons.

It is clear that every photographic reproduction tends to some extent to be subjective. In our case, too, the African masks are presented in the manner they were seen by the two authors of this book, particularly the photographer Jindřich Marco. I should like to take this opportunity to thank him for his appreciation of African art and his endless patience with which he dealt with all my wishes. My gratitude further goes out to Mrs. Jindřiška Marcová for the care with which she attended to the layout of this book.

I am indebted to Mr. W. Fagg of the British Museum for valuable information, likewise to Mrs. H. Van Geluwe of the Musée Royal de l'Afrique Centrale at Tervuren, Mr. A. D. Tushingham of the Royal Ontario Museum in Toronto and to my friend Dr. S. Wolf, Director of the Staatliches Museum für Völkerkunde in Dresden, for his help in acquiring specialist literature. I should like to acknowledge my thanks to Dr. N. Frýd and Dr. L. Jisl of Prague, the National Gallery in Prague and the City Museum in Telč for their understanding and kindness in lending the masks in their possession, which are reproduced in this book.

BIBLIOGRAPHY

Art d'Afrique dans les collections Belges, Tervuren, 1963.

Bascom, W. R. & Gebauer, Paul: *Handbook of West African Art*, Milwaukee, 1953.

Drost, Dietrich, Hans Damm & Werner Hartwig: *Ornament und Plastik fremder Völker*, Leipzig, 1964.

Elisofon, Eliot & Fagg, William: *The Sculpture of Africa*, London, 1958.

Fagg, William: *Africa: 100 Tribus—100 chefs d'oeuvre*, Berlin, 1964.

Fagg, William: *The Webster Plass Collection*, London, 1953.

Het Masker: Alle volken—Alle tijden, Antwerp, 1956.

Himmelheber, Hans: *Negerkunst und Negerkünstler*, Brunswick, 1960.

Krieger, Kurt & Gerdt Kutscher: *Westafrikanische Masken*, Berlin, 1960.

Leuzinger, Elsy: *Africa: the Art of the Negro Peoples*, London, 1962.

Leuzinger, Elsy: *Afrikanische Skulptur*, Museum Rietberg, Zürich, 1963.

Olbrechts, Frans M.: *Les Arts plastiques du Congo Belge*, Brussels, 1959.

Riley, Olive L.: *Masks and Magic*, New York, 1955.

Schweeger-Hafel, A.: *Holzplastik in Afrika*, Vienna, 1960.

Segy, Ladislas: *African Sculpture Speaks*, New York, 1961.

Sydow, Eckart von: *Afrikanische Plastik*, Berlin, 1954.

Underwood, Leon: *Masks of West Africa*, London, 1948.

Vatican Exhibition. *The Arts in Belgian Congo and Ruanda-Urundi*, Brussels, 1950

Detailed bibliographical data on African art can be found in the main general works included in this bibliography. Other masks in Czech collections were published in the book by W. and B. Forman: *Exotic Art*, Artia, Prague, 1956.

DESCRIPTION OF THE PLATES

SIERRA LEONE AND LIBERIA

1

Helmet mask of light-coloured soft wood, dyed dark brown on the surface and inside. The face is conceived in the shape of a small triangle set on one corner which forms a miniature mouth that projects slightly. The hair is indicated in the shape of several crests that spread fan-wise from the centre of the top of the head. The folds at the neck indicate fatness which was considered a mark of beauty in a woman. The mask was worn by a member of the secret women's society of Bundu or Sande during initiation ceremonies.
Mende tribe, Sierra Leone or Liberia.
Former collection of J. Hloucha.
h. 40 cm.; w. 21.5 cm.　　　　　No. 39109

2

Flat mask of light-coloured wood, dyed dark brown with red and white polychrome horns and ornaments on the forehead. The flat piece between the horns bears three broad, flat notches to which originally further ornaments, now lost, were attached. Along the sides, at the height of the eyes, are two similar notches where the ears had probably been attached. They are now also lost. Along the edge of the lower part at the back of the mask are seventeen tiny holes to which fringes or costume had been attached. The mask was perhaps worn on the forehead or the top of the head horizontally, since it has no holes for eyes. In shape and simplicity of expression it is close to published Landa masks of the Toma tribe (see Segy, *African Sculpture Speaks*, p. 166), but it differs in the lightness and delicacy of execution (W. Fagg in a letter to the author).
Toma tribe (?), Liberia or Sierra Leone.
Former collection of J. Maternová.
h. 64 cm. (without horns 41 cm.); w. 24 cm.　　　　　No. A 844

IVORY COAST

3

Face mask of light-coloured wood, dyed black, with shiny patina. Characteristic features include the oval shape, arched forehead and a horizontal groove in which the eyes are set. The circular eye holes are outlined with a ring of aluminium foil, and the teeth partly covering the oval mouth hole are made of the same material. A strip of red cotton material is stuck onto the upper lip. The mask has tiny holes along its edge where the costume must have been attached.

This mask was worn by village officials whose responsibility it was to guard against fire during periods of drought and when a fire broke out to warn the villagers working in the fields (E. Leuzinger, *Afrikanische Skulptur*).

Dan tribe, Ivory Coast.
Former collection of J. Maternová.
h. 21 cm.; w. 13 cm.   No. A 846

4

Face mask of light-coloured wood, dyed brown-black. By its shape, the typical features of face modelling and the quiet conception this mask belongs to the style of the Dan tribe. The edge that outlines the face, the stress on the lower lip and perhaps the concave ridge of the nose are probably local stylistic features, possibly those of a particular ethnic group.

Dan tribe, Ivory Coast.
Formerly in the Mission Museum of the Monastery at Teplice-Bohosudov, western Bohemia.
h. 24.5 cm.; w. 14 cm.   No. 39464

5

Miniature mask with handle, made of heavy, light-coloured wood, dyed brown with a shiny patina. In form it has all the features typical of the large masks of the Dan tribe: an oval shape, comparatively high, domed forehead with a vertical scar in the centre, a sharp groove in which the eyes are set and Cubist modelling of the cheeks as if composed of horizontally placed three-sided prisms.

These masks were used by village magicians (H. Himmelheber, *Negerkunst und Negerkünstler*, p. 161).

Dan tribe, Ivory Coast.

Former collection of J. Hloucha, acquired in 1936.

h. 14.5 cm.; w. 6.5 cm.   No. 26575

6—7

Face mask of brown wood with dark-brown patina, and on the lower part of the face, from the eye holes to the chin, remnants of dark-red earth dye. Along the circumference of the tubular eyes there are remnants of resin; the mouth holds four animal teeth. Along the edge of the mask is a row of holes to which, along the lower half, a collar of cock feathers is attached.

The cylindrical eyes are probably typical of the Ngere tribe which, together with the Dan, make up a wider stylistic province.

Dan-Ngere tribe, Ivory Coast.

Former collection of J. Hloucha, acquired in 1950.

h. (without feather collar) 26 cm.; w. 15 cm.   No. 39397

33

8

Face mask of light-coloured wood, with brown-black patina. A thick layer of white colour is to be found on the lower side of the projecting forehead, the strip below the forehead, and the edge of the cylindrical eye holes. On the narrow forehead, the nose and the lower lip there is dark-red colour below the layer of patina. The eye cylinders are open at the back, but the bearer of the mask looked through two sets of slits above and below the eye cylinders. Two (originally probably four) iron teeth are attached to the mouth and the tongue, stuck in, is made of red cotton material. A string beard is attached to the edge of the mask and the beard on the chin is made of human hair.

This mask has features of the Dan tribal style (especially in the modelling of the cheeks, conceived as horizontal three-sided prisms), but the predominating features are those of the Ngere tribe—the low, strongly projecting forehead, the cylindrical eyes, the overall awe-inspiring appearance.

Dan-Ngere tribe, Ivory Coast.

Former collection of J. Hloucha, acquired in 1936.

h. (without beard) 24.5 cm.; w. 11.5 cm.   No. 26571

9

Face mask of light-coloured wood, coloured grey-brown, with a shiny surface. The nose is flat, its edge concave, the cylindrical opaque eyes are set below an arch, probably developed by joining the two horn-shaped rims along the side of the mask, typical of the style of the Ngere tribe (compare plate 11). The actual slits for the eyes are placed in a deep groove below the strongly domed forehead. A vertical scar runs down the centre of the forehead. This occurs likewise among masks of the Dan tribe. The mouth holds six teeth of ceramic splinters covered in white glaze. A 'mane' or beard of bast is attached along the edge of the mask.

Style of the Ngere tribe, region of the Sassandra River, Ivory Coast.

Collected by Dr. J. Golovin, acquired in 1935.

h. (without beard) 29 cm.; w. 19.5 cm.   No. 7617

10

Face mask of light-coloured wood with black surface dye. Two pairs of slits are to be found at the root of the nose. The two arches above the face and the tusks at the corner of the stylized relief-shaped mouth are made of separate pieces of wood and attached to the mask with iron nails. Remnants of fur can be seen on the low forehead. Originally it must have lined the face in narrow stripes along the sides. A 'mane' or beard of bast is attached to the edge of the mask.

Style of the Ngere tribe, region of the Sassandra River, Ivory Coast.

Collected by Dr. J. Golovin, acquired in 1935.

h. (without beard) 30 cm.; w. 19 cm.   No. 7649

11

Face mask of light-coloured soft wood, its surface coloured dark-brown. White paint is found on the projecting parts of the face. A pair of small slits at the root of the nose served for viewing. Three pairs of small holes are placed along the side of the nose, one above the other, but covered with strands of plant fibres. The geometrically placed holes in the cylindrical projections are shallow. The animal mouth holds sixteen pairs of wooden teeth. Two of the four horn-shaped projections are broken off. Along the edge of the mask can be found a beard of plant fibre attached with wooden pegs.

The collector is said to have acquired this mask from a witch-doctor who used it during treatment.

Style of the Ngere tribe, cercle Daloa, Ivory Coast.

Collected by Dr. J. Golovin, acquired in 1935.

h. (without beard) 33 cm.; w. 26 cm.   No. 7615

12

Animal mask of light-coloured wood, with a shiny polychrome black and white surface. Masks of this type were worn horizontally on the top of the head. Like this example, they link different animal and human features in one organic unit. Although the collector gave for provenance the Bete tribe, this mask, in conception and style, belongs to the Senufo tribe living further north, mainly on account of its long narrow nose with slightly widened nostrils at the end.

Among the Senufo tribe these masks were used during ceremonies to drive away magic.

Bete tribe, Gagnoa subdivision, Ivory Coast (according to collector's data).

Collected by Dr. J. Golovin, acquired in 1935.

h. 37 cm.; w. 19 cm.   No. 7627

13

Face mask of light-coloured wood, painted black, light-brown, red and white, with a thick layer of patina on the outside and inside. The hair and beard are made of monkey (?) fur, narrow strips of animal skin are attached to the edge of the upper eyelids. Originally they must have had fur and served in the place of eyelashes. Along the edge of the mask is a row of tiny holes through which a string has been threaded which held the fringes or garment. At the height of the lower lids a bar is attached to the inner walls of the mask which bears tooth marks.

A similar example was on show at the exhibition *Art d'Afrique dans les collections Belges* in the Musée Royal de l'Afrique Centrale, Tervuren, 1963, exhibition catalogue No. 378, belonging to the collection of R. Vander Straete, Brussels. Originally it formed part of the Sandro Volta collection.

Guro tribe, Ivory Coast.

Exhibited at the World Exhibition of African Art in Dakar and Pa is, 1966, exhibition catalogue No. 132.

h. 29.5 cm.; w. 20 cm.   No. A 2844

14

Face mask of light-coloured wood, painted black, red and white, linking animal and human features in one organic unit. The horn-shaped projections represent stylized antelope horns. The curve of the profile of the mask, the high arched forehead and small animal mouth, identical with those of well-known antelope masks of the Guro tribe, make it possible to attribute this mask to that region. This is further upheld by a bar joining the sides of the mask at the back, at the height of the mouth of its wearer, who held it by his teeth. In most of the masks of the Guro tribe there are at least holes to which these bars had originally been attached. Along the edge of the mask a row of holes served to attach the costume.

Guro tribe, Gagnoa subdivision, Ivory Coast.
Collected by Dr. J. Golovin, acquired in 1935.
h. 40 cm.; w. 23.5 cm.   No. 7652

15

Face mask of light-coloured wood, painted white, brown-red and black, with anthropo-zoomorphic features, similar to the preceding mask, in style likewise typical of the Guro tribe, but showing a larger measure of abstraction and stylization than is normal in that style. A pair of large holes are burnt into the upper edge of the side walls to which a bar was attached for holding the mask by the teeth. Therefore the narrow slits probably did not serve the wearer to see out from.

Style of the Guro tribe, Gagnoa subdivision, Ivory Coast.
Collected by Dr. J. Golovin, acquired in 1935.
h. 40 cm.; w. 17.5 cm.   No. 7626

37

16—17

Face mask of light-coloured wood, painted in brown-red and white. The line of the hair border, eyebrows, tattooing and mouth are outlined in poker-work. Along the edge of the hollow face of the mask two pairs of holes have been burnt for fixing a bar, or probably some alternative way of supporting the mask, since the customary one pair of holes was insufficient on account of the relatively great weight of the pole-shaped attachment. The mask is of the same provenance as the preceding one and was probably made by the same carver. There is a striking contrast between the abstract conception of the mask and the realistic depiction of the head on the attached pole.

Style of the Guro tribe, Gagnoa subdivision, Ivory Coast.

Collected by Dr. J. Golovin, acquired in 1935.

h. 69 cm.; w. 16 cm.   No. 7623

18—19

Face mask of light-coloured wood, coloured black. The inner side and the ball-shaped head-dress bears marks of dark-red paint. There are slits for the eyes below the closed lids. This mask lacks some of the most striking attributes of the masks known from the Senufo tribe, yet some of its features support this attribution — mainly the long narrow nose and the treatment of the eyes.

Senufo tribe (?), Ivory Coast or Mali.

Former collection of J. Hloucha.

h. 38.5 cm.; w. 14.8 cm.   No. 39157

20

Face mask of light-coloured wood, coloured black on the outside. The horn-shaped crest above the centre of the forehead, the mouth and all grooves and scars on the cheeks are dark brownish-red. The eyes have horizontal slits. Along the edge of the mask there are four holes by which the mask was attached to the head. This mask has all the characteristic features of this type of Senufo mask: a long, narrow nose, a double groove above the eyes, scars on the forehead, a small projecting mouth, wing-shaped projections along the sides and a couple of vertical protuberances at the bottom of the mask, which perhaps represent rudimentary legs.

These masks were used during funeral ceremonies of the Lo Society. All authors agree that masks of this kind have now been degraded to the level of souvenirs. Nonetheless, some of the recent products possess undoubted artistic quality.

Senufo tribe, Ivory Coast.

Former collection of J. Maternová.

h. 27.5 cm.; w. 17 cm.   No. A 1693

21

Face mask of light-coloured wood, coloured black, with patina. The large eye holes are set in a deep horizontal groove below the domed forehead with the characteristic vertical cicatrice which give masks of this type a particular expression of thoughtfulness. Six long, thin pieces of string inserted in the chin form a beard.

Style of the Guro tribe, area of the Sassandra River, Ivory Coast.

Collected by Dr. J. Golovin, acquired in 1935.

h. 28 cm.; w. 15.5 cm.   No. 7654

22

Face mask of white wood, coloured grey-brown, remnants of a white colouring matter can be found on the horizontal stripe around the eyes and along the sides. Remnants of red colour remain in the grooves of the scarification on the forehead and those indicating hair. There are narrow slits in the eyes, the mouth holds two iron teeth, and the beard is made of string.

Although in contrast to the preceding masks this one is worked in rougher manner and tends to subdivide the face into geometrical elements, it is related in certain features of style: the domed forehead with the vertical scarification in the centre, the horizontal groove at the height of the upper edge of the eyes, and the small mouth with teeth of different material. The collector, too, gave the same provenance.

Area of the Sassandra River, Ivory Coast.
Collected by Dr. J. Golovin, acquired in 1935.
h. (without beard) 30 cm.; w. 19 cm.   No. 7659

23

Face mask of light-coloured soft wood, coloured brown, with patina, and no eye slits. Large iron nails form the irises of the eyes. Into the crest-shaped hairstyle is fixed a long hanging plait, braided, of the fair hair of a European woman. The vertical scarification on the domed forehead, the eyes set in horizontal grooves in the centre of the mask, the small mouth projecting forward and the teeth (with filed central incisors), the small ears and the general appearance make it possible to ascribe this mask to the style of the Guro tribe.

Style of the Guro tribe, area of the Sassandra River, Ivory Coast.
Collected by Dr. J. Golovin, acquired in 1935.
h. 39 cm.; w. 20.5 cm.   No. 7656

24

Animal mask of light-coloured wood with grey-brown shiny patina, worn horizontally on the top of the head.

This highly abstract mask shows an animal head in abstract spherical forms and represents a figure from the mythology of the Baule tribe, the demi-god Guli (buffalo). It was used to drive away demons and magic powers. By contrast to known Guli masks of the Baule tribe, this example is smaller and has no polychromy. The raised ridge on the vertical axis of the mask is smooth and sharp, without the usual notches, and the horns are smooth and flattened.

Baule tribe (?), cercle Daloa, Ivory Coast.

Collected by Dr. J. Golovin, acquired in 1935.

h. 39.5 cm.; w. 17.5 cm.　　　　　　　No. 7671

NIGERIA

25—26

Mask of light-coloured wood, painted red-brown, black, white and blue which is found in remnants between the three strips of cowrie shells above the forehead. Circular pupils are burnt into the eyes; in the nose are triangular holes which might have served for vision. A white lip-plug is fixed in the lower lip.

Masks of this type are a typical product of the Yoruba-speaking people living in south-western Nigeria and in the neighbouring countries to the west. They are worn by members of the male Gelede Society during annual celebrations, and funerals of their members. Typical features of the masks are their semi-circular or semi-egg-shaped form adapted for wearing on the top of the head or the forehead. The eyes of the masks are always open, the lips parallel, cut away at the ends, without corners, and many of the masks have tribal scarification marks on the forehead and cheeks, taking the form of three parallel scars. During celebrations these masks appear in identical pairs.

Yoruba, Nigeria.

Former collection of A. Sachs, acquired in 1926.

h. 36 cm.; w. 19.5 cm.　　　　　　　No. 23482

41

27

Double mask of light-coloured wood, painted grey-white and black; the ribbon on the back of the hairstyle is red-brown, blue and white. Circular pupils are burnt into the eyes, but they do not go through into the concave part of the mask. Two real eye-holes are hidden under the chins of the two faces, which indicates that the masks were worn on the forehead. Along the edge at the height of the temples there are two holes by which the masks were attached to the head.
Yoruba, Nigeria.
Former collection of A. Sachs, acquired in 1926.
h. 36.5 cm.; w. 26 cm.   No. 23467

28

Mask of light-coloured wood, painted yellow-white, black, yellow, white, blue and red-brown. A striking feature is the light blue of the eyes. The polychromy has almost vanished. By contrast to other Yoruba masks this example has no tribal marks on the forehead and cheeks. Circular pupils are burnt into the eyes, the nostrils are triangular.
Yoruba, Nigeria.
Former collection of A. Sachs, acquired in 1926.
h. 42 cm.; w. 20.5 cm.   No. 23496

29

Mask of hard, light-coloured wood, painted yellow-white, blue, black and red-brown. This mask, too, has light blue of the eyes. As in the preceding one, circular pupils are burnt into the eyes, and the large triangular nostrils probably served for vision. One of the originally five vertical protuberances above the forehead is broken off.
Yoruba, Nigeria.
Former collection of A. Sachs, acquired in 1926.
h. 38.5 cm.; w. 25 cm.   No. 23468

30

Mask of light-coloured wood, painted blue, white, black and red-brown. Although this mask shows all the features prescribed for the canon of Yoruba art, it differs from the preceding masks in the conception of individual parts of the face and the manner of treatment. The eyes in the preceding masks stood out from the head plastically in such a manner that when seen from below they would give a frontal view. This is not the case in this mask. Here, too, holes have been burnt into the eyes to serve as pupils, but the eyes themselves have the shape of half-moons turned with the open side towards the forehead. The nose is longer and its ridge is sharp. The lips are slightly open and do not form two parallel lines, as in the case of other masks. The tribal scarification marks are indicated merely in paint, not carved in relief. The carving of the mask is rougher and the details of the face do not form such a harmonious unit of rounded curves and projecting areas as on the preceding masks.
Yoruba, Nigeria.
Former collection of A. Sachs, acquired in 1926.
h. 32 cm.; w. 22 cm.   No. 23485

43

31—32

Mask of light-coloured wood, painted pink, blue, black, red-brown and white. Circular holes are burnt into the eyes for pupils, but the function of vision is probably provided by the triangular nostrils. The top of the head is adorned with the figure of a bird fighting a snake, and along the sides are two small stylized figures of tortoises. This mask and the subsequent one differ from the preceding Yoruba masks. The shape is more rounded and the face shorter and narrower. The eyes project only slightly from the face and are stressed in outline. The nose is shorter to fit into the general conception of the mask and hardly projects at all from the face. The parallel lines of tribal marks on the cheeks are elongated downwards.
Yoruba, Nigeria or Dahomey (?).
Former collection of A. Sachs, acquired in 1926.
h. 46 cm.; w. 24 cm.   No. 23469

33

Mask of light-coloured wood, painted pink, blue, black, red-brown and white. This mask was probably made by the same artist who made the preceding one.
Yoruba, Nigeria or Dahomey (?).
Former collection of A. Sachs, acquired in 1926.
h. 32.5 cm.; w. 23 cm.   No. 23464

44

34

Mask of light-coloured wood, dyed brown. The subdivided straight face with its geometrical shapes indicates provenance from the eastern parts of the Niger Delta.

The shape of the mask is adapted to its function. It probably represents a water spirit and was worn on the top of the head in a horizontal position during Owu games, like the better-known masks in the form of stylized hippopotamus heads. The bearer of the mask was submerged in the water to be seen by the spectators from above. This mask, however, lacks all documentation and its function and provenance can only be deduced from its shape and from similar masks.

The ends of the four protuberances on the top of the head are broken off. It is quite possible that originally they were linked and formed a more complex decoration or symbolic form.

Kalabari Ijo tribe (?), Niger Delta.
Former collection of J. Maternová.
h. 61.5 cm.; w. 19.8 cm.   No. A 842

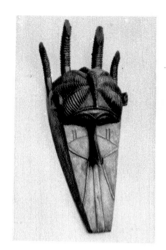

35

Mask of light-coloured wood, covered in antelope skin dyed yellow and black. The eyes are covered in aluminium foil attached at the pupils with iron nails, the mouth holds teeth carved from bone. Masks of this type were worn by members of secret societies during various ceremonies of the Ekkpe cult.
Ekoi tribe, Cross River area, S.-E. Nigeria or Cameroons.
Former collection of A. Sachs, acquired in 1926.
h. 61 cm.; w. 36 cm.   No. 23527

36—37

Mask of light-coloured wood, covered in antelope skin dyed yellow and black. The eyes are covered in aluminium foil attached at the pupils with iron nails. The open mouth holds two rows of wooden teeth. As in the preceding mask, the neck is attached to a woven cap-shaped mat, since these masks were worn on the top of the head.

Masks of this kind belong to the naturalistic art from the Cross River area. The Ekoi tribe in the Cameroons is usually given as provenance. They applied this style in its purest form. But some masks and sculptures that can be shown to have been made by the Ekoi tribe are more naturalistic: for example, they have real human hair attached, while in the case of our mask the hair is replaced by wooden pegs or the scalp is painted black. Typical of this group are the hairstyles in the form of horns or spirals. A very similar mask was published by W. R. Bascom and Paul Gebauer in their *Handbook of West African Art*, Milwaukee 1953, p. 53, where they give the Efik, a sub-tribe of the Ibibio, living along the lower reaches of the Cross River, south of the Ekoi as provenance. The mask belongs to the Royal Ontario Museum, Toronto, and in the catalogue is attributed to the Ekoi tribe (cat. no. 935.10.1). H. Himmelheber attributes such masks to the Ibibio tribe, the western neighbours of the Ekoi on Nigerian territory.

Ekoi tribe, Cross River area, S.-E. Nigeria or Cameroons.
Former collection of A. Sachs, acquired in 1926.
h. 63 cm.; w. 43 cm.   No. 23528

GABOON

38

Face mask of light-coloured wood, painted white, black and red. The eyes are piereced with curved slits. The shape of the eyes, one of the most striking features of the masks, gave cause for consideration of its provenance. These masks strikingly resemble Japanese theatrical masks and some scholars suggested that Javanese masks might have served as patterns for the masks from Gaboon. Such a theory is further upheld by the small concave nose and the white colour of the face, which, however, in Africa is a normal feature of the world of spirits. Other reasons, too, indicate that the similarity to Oriental masks is accidental. Typical features on these masks include scarification on the temples and particularly on the forehead, made from small scars placed in squares or vertical lines in the centre of the forehead. Some of these masks, however, lack this scarification. The hairstyle is usually composed of three, sometimes more lobes turned towards the sideways axis of the mask. It represents the spirit of a dead woman who has returned from the world of the dead. The bearer of the mask walks on stilts while appearing in this mask.

M'Pongwe or Balumbo tribe, Gaboon.
Collected by A. David in the first half of this century.
h. 27.5 cm.; w. 16.5 cm.   No. 39238

39—40

Face mask of pale-coloured lightweight wood, painted white and brown, with straight slits in the eyes. The fairly rare asymmetrical shape of this mask gives it the character of an individual portrait. H. Himmelheber records from the Masango, a tribe of southern Gaboon among whom masks of this kind are found, how a local carver related to him that he used the face of one of the nicest living girls as a model for the masks.

M'Pongwe or Balumbo tribe, Gaboon.
Collected by A. David in the first half of this century.
h. 25 cm.; w. 13.5 cm.   No. 39237

CAMEROONS

41

Face mask of light brown hardwood, coloured dark on the outside, with large eye holes and wide holes in the nose and ears. The walls of the mask are relatively thin and the hollow for the face is consequently very roomy. Typical stylistic features are the full cheeks, the small pointed chin and the relatively large ear lobes. The large variety of these masks led to the assumption that they portrayed individual persons. The masks were worn during various ceremonies such as new moon celebrations and funerals of the King.

Along the edge of the mask are six holes, to which fringes or clothes were attached.

Bamileke tribe, Cameroons Grasslands.

Private collection of L. Jisl, Prague.

h. 34 cm.; w. 27 cm.

42

Helmet mask of light-coloured wood, coloured dark brown, carved in the same technique as the preceding mask. At the back of the head there is the same decoration as at the front of the mask. A circular hole is found on the top.

Bekom tribe (?), Cameroons Grasslands.

Former collection of J. Maternová.

h. 38.5 cm.; w. 24 cm.   No. A 843

43

Animal mask of light-coloured wood, coloured dark brown on the outside. The eyes are outlined in grooves and contrast the natural colour of the wood against the dyed surface of the mask. These masks represent buffaloes; they were worn horizontally on the top of the head and used during dances before setting off on a hunt.
The cavity at the back is usually divided into two parts by a wall that was left during the carving of the mask.
Bamileke tribe, Cameroons Grasslands.
Private collection of N. Frýd, Prague.
h. 77 cm.; w. 32.5 cm.

44

Face mask of light brown hardwood, with red-brown patina, hair and beard made of string into which human hair has been plaited. This mask clearly shows a characteristic feature of this style of masks from the Cameroons Grasslands, namely the frozen smile.
Bamum tribe (?), Cameroons Grasslands.
Former collection of J. Hloucha, acquired in 1936.
h. 41 cm.; w. 29 cm.　　　　　No. 26583

49

CONGO

45

Face mask of light-coloured wood, painted brown and black. The back part of the hair is woven of string and loose raffia fibre. Along the edge of the face are small openings with remnants of string by which the mask was tied to the garment. In the left ear and originally also in the right one there is a pendant of tiny red glass beads. The eyes and mouth are pierced with narrow horizontal slits.

The most important stylistic feature of this dancing mask from the Bajokwe tribe of the southern Congo and Angola are the eyes shaped like coffee-beans, set in larger or smaller concave hollows. The hair covered with parallel grooves in the shape of a turban is another characteristic feature. This hairstyle is known from older figure sculptures of the tribe. The long slightly widening nose is also characteristic.

The mask represents a woman, but it was worn by men and the garments woven of plant fibres included breasts.

Bajokwe tribe, Angola or southern Congo.

h. 24.5 cm.; w. 19.5 cm.   No. 4658

46

Face mask of light-coloured hardwood with brown-red surface. The typical ellipsoidal eyes are pierced with slits. Characteristic of the Bajokwe tribe is the tattooing on the forehead, shaped as a cross made up of a square and four triangles and the asymmetrical tattooing on the cheeks. The hair of plaited plant fibre served to cover the head of the wearer. The knots on the top of the head recall the hairstyle worn by the women of the Bajokwe tribe, where similar knots are formed with the help of mud.

Bajokwe tribe, southern Congo.

Collected by F. V. Foit in 1949.

h. 21 cm.; w. 11 cm.   No. 27922

47

Face mask of light-coloured hardwood with black surface. The eyes are narrow slits, the mouth holds two (originally three) wooden teeth, and tufts of animal fur on the corners of the mouth and the chin are attached with wax to represent a beard. The cheeks show scarification in the form of five dots forming a cross.

Although this mask is rather unusual, it retains all elements of style of the Bajokwe tribe.

Bajokwe tribe, southern Congo.

Collected by F. V. Foit in 1949.

h. 28.5 cm.; w. 21 cm.   No. 27921

48

Face mask made of basket-work covered with rough fabric onto which a crude schematic face is modelled in a black compound (probably resin and wax). The parts of eyes below the continuous horizontal brow ridge are painted with a band of pink. The face shows tattooing in the form of four circular holes set in a square; the mouth holds two (originally four) teeth. The top of the head is covered in wild cat and monkey fur. The back and neck of the wearer of the mask were covered by a veil made of raffia and cotton string. Inside the mask at the height of the mouth a small wind instrument is attached designed to produce super-natural sounds.

Masks of this type were worn in camps in the bush where young boys were prepared for initiation.

Bajokwe tribe, southern Congo.

Collected by F. V. Foit in 1950.

h. 32 cm.; w. 20 cm.   No. 43662

49

Face mask constructed of basket-work covered with rough fabric (hessian). The face part is covered with a layer of plastic black mixture as on the preceding mask, facial features are graphically expressed, with white and dark-red cotton strips attached to the surface. The lower and upper side of the gigantic headdress, made of rough fabric stretched on basketwork, is decorated with geometrical ornament in white triangles picked out in a thick layer of chalk colouring.

These masks were worn by the guards of the camps in the bush where young boys were educated for initiation. Their purpose was to drive away women.

Bajokwe tribe, southern Congo.

Collected by F. V. Foit in 1950.

h. (face only) 26 cm.; w. 22.5 cm., maximum diameter of head-dress 76 cm. No. 39164

50

Face mask of yellow-white wood, painted white, yellow and black. This mask has certain elements of the style of the Bakuba tribe in the Kassai province. First of all, the broad nose with nostrils emphasized by arch-shaped notches, and distinguished even in colour; the bridge linking nose and mouth and the abstract conception of the mouth which corresponds in width to the nostrils. Another characteristic feature is the line that outlines the forehead and hair, which is found more frequently on sculptures. The conical eyes set in deep hollows are typical of this type of mask which was used by the Babende secret society. They carried out police functions.

This mask, lacking all slits for vision, was probably made for the souvenir market rather than for traditional use. It is interesting since it combines all the main elements of the Bakuba style with a non-traditional combination of colours.

Bakuba tribe, carved by Sefryano. Congo.

Collected by F. V. Foit at Mushenge in 1950.

h. 31 cm.; w. 22 cm. No. 43650

52

51

Face mask of light-coloured wood, painted white, red-brown and grey-black. In addition to the triangular ornament, masks of this type have conical eyes with perforations along the edge. The slanting lines on the face are also typical of Bakuba masks. The conical shape of the mouth is in harmony with that of the eyes and raises the artistic value of this mask, but it is likely to be an innovation.

The function of this mask is identical to that of the preceding one.

Bakuba tribe, carved by Mikobi Louis. Congo.
Collected by F. V. Foit at Mushenge in 1950.
h. 29.7 cm.; w. 18 cm.   No. 43647

52

Example of the carver's method in producing helmet masks of the 'bombo' type (compare plate 54).
Bakuba tribe, carved by Sefryano. Congo.
Collected by F. V. Foit at Mushenge in 1950.
h. 28 cm.; w. 28 cm.   No. 43665

53

53—54

Helmet mask of light-coloured wood with black surface. The forehead, mouth and the two characteristic strips lying across the cheeks are covered in copper foil, the face is decorated with strips of raffia fabric onto which multicoloured beads are sewn. At the back the glass beads form a geometrical ornament. The large hole at the top of the mask is covered with a raffia fabric, with loosely hanging goat (?) hair attached to the edge. Cowrie shells and rattles of plant seeds are sewn onto the lower edge of the mask. In the middle of the chin a long fur beard is attached, with a few elephant hairs woven into its edge. This mask called 'bombo' was used during initiation ceremonies and, in the view of some authors, its strongly domed forehead was derived from the physiognomy of the pygmies.
Bakuba tribe, carved by Sefryano. Congo.
Collected by F. V. Foit at Mushenge in 1950.
h. 28 cm.; w. 28 cm.   No. 43664

55

Helmet mask made of basket-work covered in raffia fabric to which cowrie shells and glass beads are sewn. The face is covered with stripes of light and dark fur designed and sewn to make up the triangular ornament typical of the polychrome masks of the Bakuba tribe. The ears and nose are carved in light-coloured wood. There are small slits below the eyes which are made of cowrie shells and glass beads. This mask has features typical of the style of the Bakuba tribe: the merging of the nose and mouth, stressed by the attachment of a strip of glass beads and the ornament imitating woven material. Such ornaments can be found on the wooden boxes of the Bakuba, on their woven fabrics and in the scarifications on the bodies of members of the

54

tribe. Masks of this type were called 'mashamboy' and represented the demon that brings disease. According to tradition the Bakuba kings used them to frighten their women.
Bakuba tribe, Congo.
Collected by F. V. Foit in 1950.
h. 45 cm.; w. 24 cm.   No. 4861

56—57

Helmet mask of wood and basket-work covered with raffia fabric. The face and the head of the bird figure at the top of the mask are carved of light-coloured wood and painted white, blue and dark red. The comparatively small face is set into a projecting rim and bears two elements characteristic of the style of masks and figure sculpture of the Bayaka tribe living in the river basin of the Kwango River in the southern Congo. The first is the more or less deformed nose, usually up-tilted and sometimes turned back in the shape of an elephant trunk, as on this mask. The origin of this deformation is not entirely clear; perhaps it resembles the beak of a certain bird. No less characteristic is the framing of the eyes and forehead by a single or double circle that starts at the bottom of the nose and joins in the centre of the forehead. In the case of polychrome masks this part is distinguished in colour from the surrounding parts.

Below the figure of the bird there are four discs decorated in pairs with the same geometrical ornaments. As in all Bayaka masks there is a projection hidden among the raffia fibres whereby the mask was held during dances.

These masks were worn by young boys who left the camp after a year in the bush and danced in them before the village people.
Bayaka tribe, Congo.
Collected by F. V. Foit in 1950.
h. 53 cm.; w. about 37 cm.   No. 4814

55

58

Helmet mask of the same type as the preceding one, with different polychromy in white, blue and yellow. A small figure of a bird is placed at the top of the mask. The eyes in the form of short cylinders differ from the traditional style of the tribe.
Bayaka tribe, Congo.
Collected by F. V. Foit in 1950.
h. 48 cm.; w. 58 cm.   No. 4818

59—60

Helmet mask constructed in similar manner to the two preceding ones, but differing in the larger size of the face and its details. The nose lacks the customary deformation, the form of the eyes is more complex. They have greatly stressed eyelids, which give the eyes a living expression. The ears are comparatively large and fan-shaped. A typical feature is the high conical head-dress with three graded discs. These features are more or less identical with other masks of this type that have been published, and which represent the highest degree in the hierarchy of masks of the boys' camps in the bush.
Bayaka tribe, Congo.
Collected by F. V. Foit in 1950.
h. 67.5 cm.; w. about 50 cm.   No. 4813

61—62

Helmet mask, constructed in a similar manner to the preceding ones. The human face here is replaced by an animal head, which is fairly rare among masks of the Bayaka. The animal head is carved out of light-coloured wood and painted white, blue and yellow. The conical top of the mask is covered in cotton fabric, with two gradual discs covered with geometrical ornament. On the front a sitting figure of a woman is attached. Her hands are raised and her body is made of fabric while the head, limbs and genitalia are carved in wood. The head and genitalia are covered with human hair.

Bayaka tribe, Congo.

Collected by F. V. Foit in 1950.

h. 56 cm.; w. (without fringes) 17 cm. No. 4820

63—65

Helmet mask of light-coloured wood, painted brown, black, red and white; inside the head cavity the surface of the wood is dark-coloured. Below the characteristic eyes shaped like coffee-beans are small slits. The forehead is domed and passes in a concave curve into the profile of the small nose. Along the edge of the cylinder of the mask a collar of short thick raffia fibre is attached in double rows of holes, set in pairs.

A characteristic feature of the wooden mask of the Basuku tribe is the figure of a bird or some quadruped creature on the top of the head.

Basuku tribe, Congo.

Collected by F. V. Foit in 1950.

h. 38 cm.; w. (without raffia collar) 21 cm. No. 27803

57

66

Helmet mask of wood and basket-work, similar to those in plates 57—61, decorated with a stylized animal figure at the top, probably a tortoise. The wooden parts are of light-coloured wood, painted white, blue and yellow. The eyes are of the characteristic coffee-bean shape.
Bayaka tribe, Congo.
Collected by F. V. Foit in 1950.
h. 45 cm.; w. about 40 cm.   No. 4815

67

Helmet mask, constructed in similar manner to the preceding ones from the Bayaka tribe. The face area is here replaced by a male figure squatting in characteristic position. The figure is carved out of light-coloured wood, painted red, white, ochre and blue. The face of the figure has features typical of the Bayaka style, with one less common feature, namely the stress on the pupils by means of shining metal nails. The blue cap (partly broken off in front), the beard and the bottle the figure is holding indicate that we are, in all likelihood, dealing with a caricature of a European soldier. The open mouth clearly shows two rows of teeth, with the two central incisors filed to a point.
Bayaka tribe, Congo.
Collected by O. Větvičková, probably in 1928.
h. 54 cm.; w. 18 cm., h. (of figure only) 29 cm.   No. A 1613

68

Face mask carved of light, weight, pale-coloured wood, painted black and red-brown. The eyes have slits. Raffia hair is attached to the mask, and down the back of the mask hangs a long conical ornament of rough fabric stuffed with raffia fibre.

This mask shows features typical of the style of the Bapende tribe living adjacent to the Bayaka in the region of the Kwango River. The face has an introvert expression caused by the drooping eyelids, the unbroken line of the eyebrows which form a broad angle above the root of the nose, the comparatively small nose with a sharp edge, slightly concave in profile, and the slight projections of the ears and chin which forms a more obtuse angle than the line of the eye brows. The scarification marks on the forehead and the mouth are carved negatively in the case of more modern masks, so that the white wood contrasts with the surrounding polychrome areas.

Bapende tribe, Congo.

Collected by F. V. Foit in 1950.

h. 25 cm.; w. 20 cm.   No. 43655

69

Helmet mask made of basket-work covered in rough fabric. The face is outlined by the attachment of a three-ply raffia string, the nose and eyes are crudely carved of pale-coloured, light-weight wood and attached to the construction of the mask with wire. Pieces of glass are attached by resin or wax to the centre of the wooden part of the eyes. The expression of a supernatural being was raised by the arch of a twig that forms a kind of insect antenna above the face.

This mask represents a rudimentary work of art which was not produced by a professional carver and probably served the same function as the well-known masks with the gigantic hairstyle which were worn among the Bajokwe tribe by the guards of the camps in the bush (compare plate 49).

Bapende tribe (?), Congo.

Collected by F. V. Foit in 1950.

h. about 37 cm.; w. about 45 cm.   No. 27925

59

70

Face mask of light-coloured wood, coloured red-brown, with a shiny patina. There are no slits in the irises which are burnt in. A certain degeneration in the art of this tribe can be observed when this is compared with plate 68, which is at least twenty years later. This one shows greater delicacy in the carving, the forehead is sharply arched, the projecting cheek bones form characteristic patches which have entirely disappeared in masks of more recent origin. The mouth is small and closed, with drooping corners. The general expression of the mask is far more arresting.

Bapende tribe, Congo.

Former collection of J. Hloucha, acquired in 1936.

h. 34 cm. (without fringe); w. 23 cm.   No. 26604

71

Face mask of light-coloured wood, painted dark red, white and black. There are no slits in the eyes. This mask has certain basic features of the style of Bapende art, but it shows the degenerating trends of recent production. An interesting feature is the beard-like extension of the long chin. According to some sources, masks with such attributes represented the chiefs.

Bapende tribe, Congo.

Collected by F. V. Foit in 1950.

h. 44 cm.; w. 22 cm.   No. 43652

72

Face mask of light-coloured wood, painted red, black and white. The basic feature of a wider area of style in the south-eastern Congo, whence this mask originated, is the narrow nose and the circular mouth set directly below it and projecting as a small truncated cone. In width it is usually identical to the nose. The principal feature of the mask is the two large white concave ovals, with small, half-moon shaped eyes with narrow slits in the centre. These eyes are typical of the style of a comparatively small tribe, the Wabembe.

Wabembe tribe, Congo.

Collected by F. V. Foit at Baraca in 1957, now in the City Museum in Telč, Moravia.

h. 51 cm.; w. 24 cm.   No. K/7

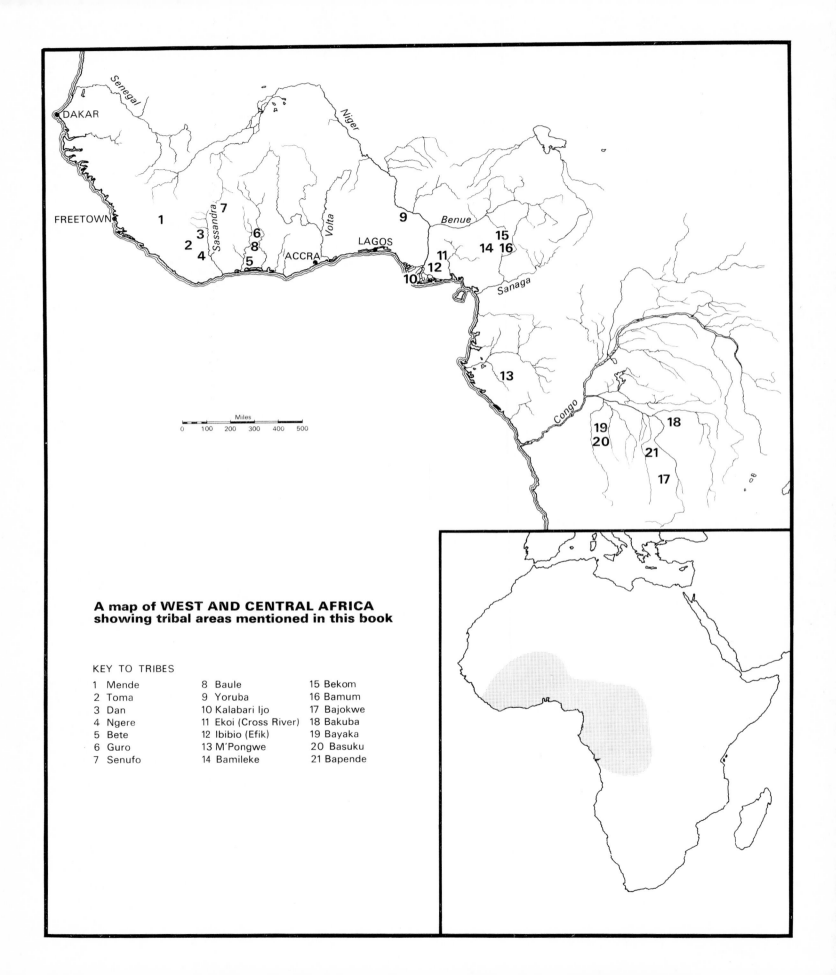

A map of **WEST AND CENTRAL AFRICA**
showing tribal areas mentioned in this book

KEY TO TRIBES

1 Mende	8 Baule	15 Bekom
2 Toma	9 Yoruba	16 Bamum
3 Dan	10 Kalabari Ijo	17 Bajokwe
4 Ngere	11 Ekoi (Cross River)	18 Bakuba
5 Bete	12 Ibibio (Efik)	19 Bayaka
6 Guro	13 M'Pongwe	20 Basuku
7 Senufo	14 Bamileke	21 Bapende

PLATES

1—72

1

2

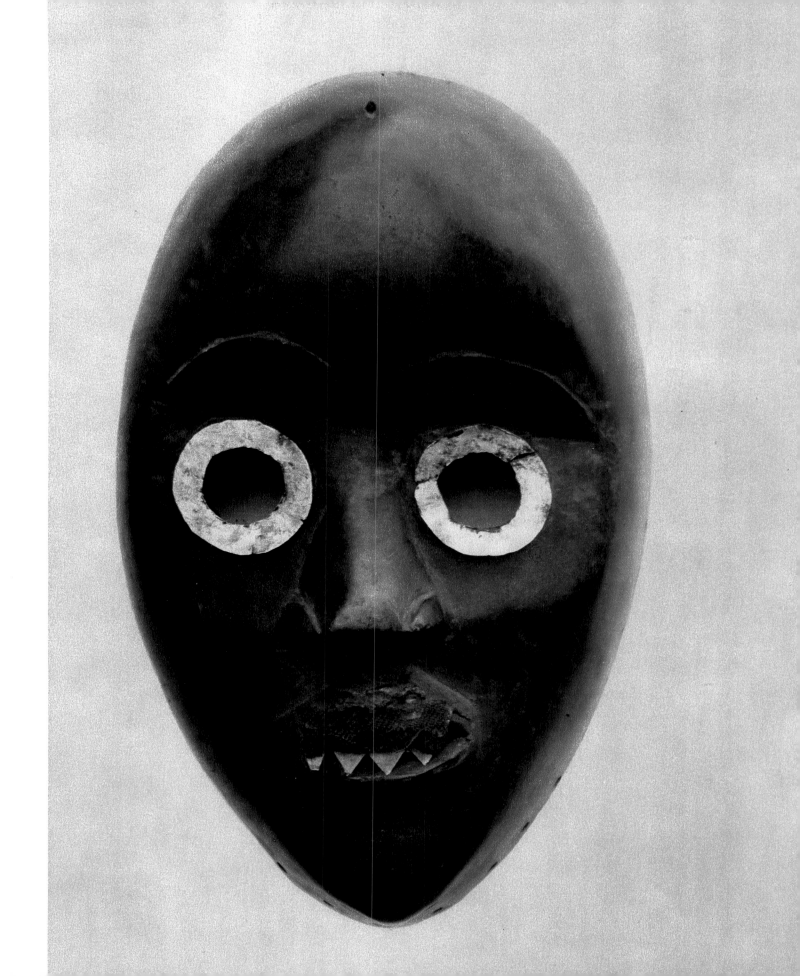

3

4

5

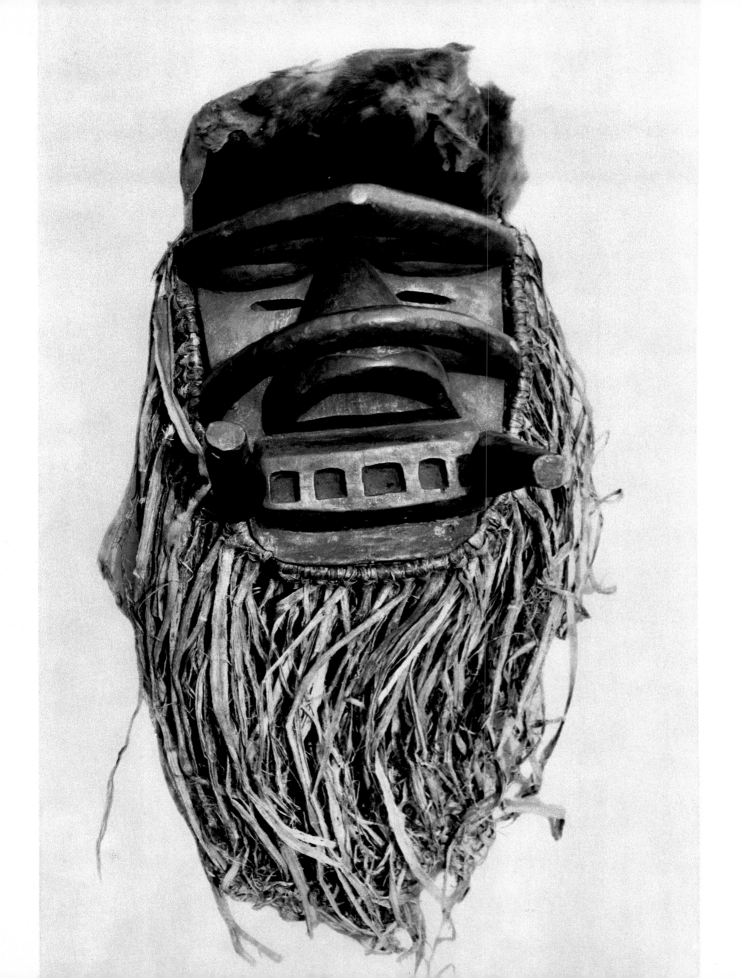

11

13

16

21

23

24

29

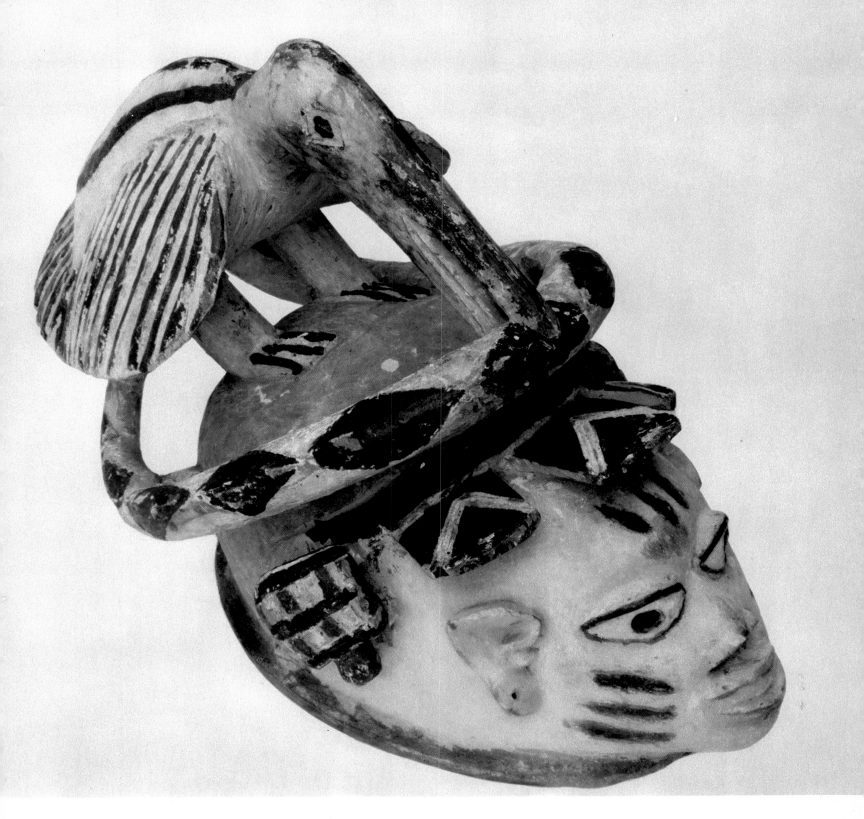

32

33

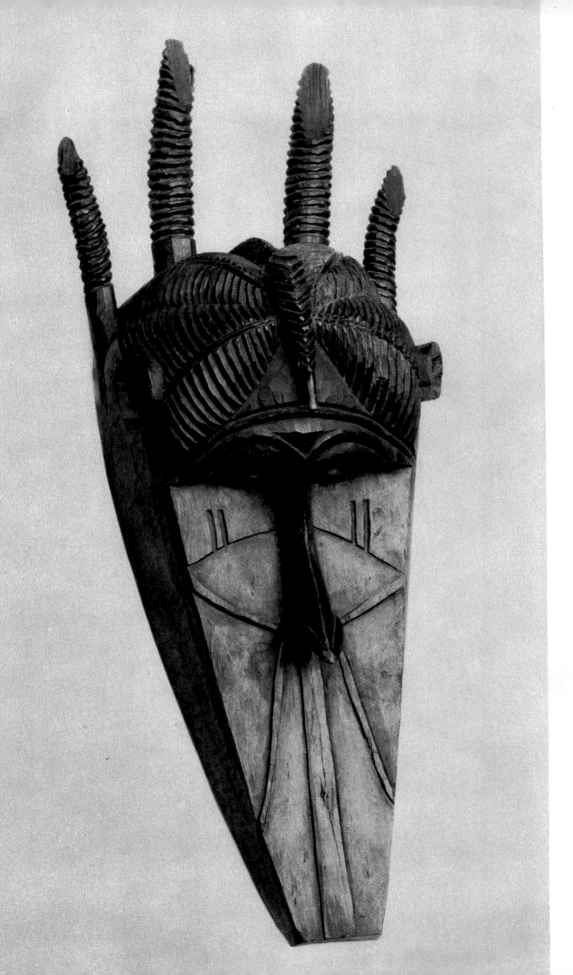

36

40

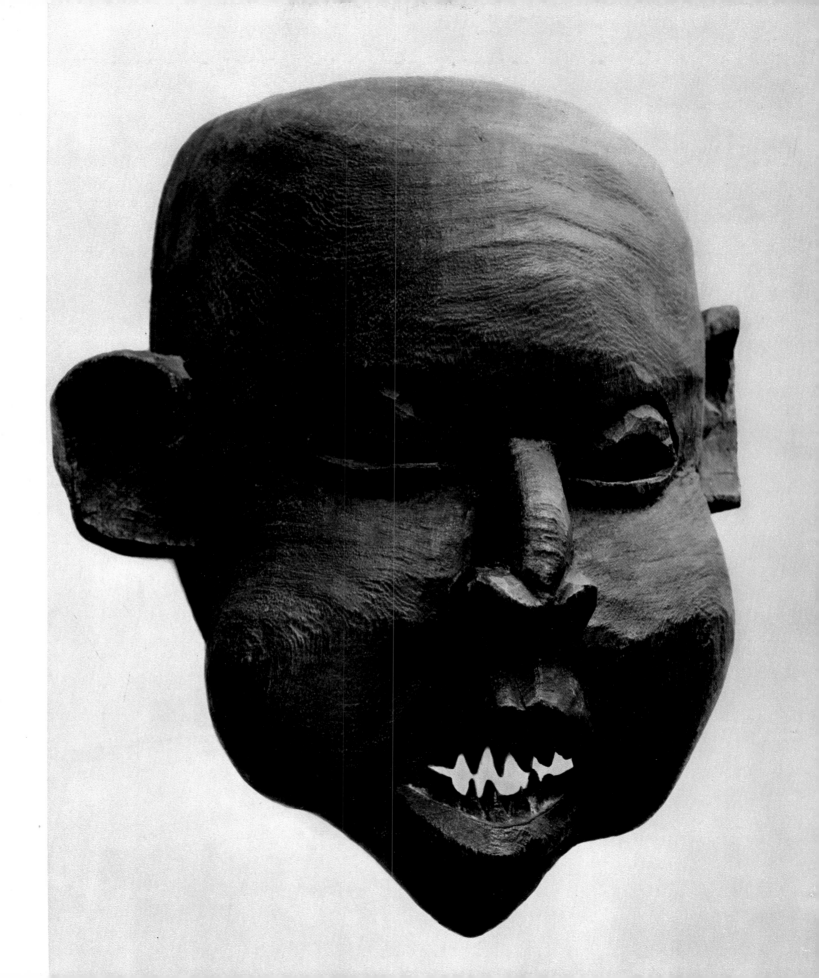

42

44

45

48

49

51